MIKROKOSMOS

Alex Comfort

SINCLAIR-STEVENSON

First published in Great Britain 1994
by Sinclair-Stevenson
an imprint of Reed Consumer Books Limited,
Michelin House, 81 Fulham Road, London SW3 6RB
and Auckland, Melbourne, Singapore and Toronto

Copyright © 1994 by Alex Comfort

ISBN 1 85619 498 1

A CIP catalogue record for this book
is available from the British Library

Typeset by Deltatype Ltd, Ellesmere Port, Cheshire
Printed and bound in Great Britain by
Cox & Wyman Ltd, Reading, Berks

Contents

For Ann, remembering Jane

In nineteen thirty-five
    I was a boy at school
studying Latin and Greek:
    it was then that I made my will

Wills look ahead, not back
    define not death but living.
We have no assets then
    and no concern with leaving

Ten pounds to the wife's niece
    and all the cutlery
to sundry relatives
    the rest to charity.

Mine was an empty sheet
    with spaces to be filled
an album without stamps,
    all the pages ruled

blank as a baby's rump
    but on each hopeful square
stood a grey replica
    of what should be stuck there.

After a year or two
    you pick your countries out:
only a bloody fool
    tries to collect the lot –

those Cape triangulars
    which stare at you in grey
aren't to be readily had
    but may turn up one day

some take a lot of work
    good luck and elbow grease:
trifles soaked from the mail
    still serve to fill a space

1

some that are overpriced –
   the stud, the genius –
and others not-worth-having
   are needed for completeness.

Reality cuts down
   the scope of the collection
to something sensible,
   a prudent expectation:

As a physician, first –
   to do more good than harm.
To take a hand at change
   and kick some fences down.

To think of some new things
   and write them legibly down:
take part of Nature apart
   and put it together again.

The lower values, too,
   rated from the beginning –
to make some solid verse:
   to sleep with many women.

Grown up, we take the thing
   and see the spaces fill.
One needs the cheek of youth
   to make a decent Will.

Often – no secret, from the verse I've written –
I have run after women
looking for love, experience, talk or pleasure,
the usual goods the sexes give each other
and have had these, but found more there
and wholly of the mind
than I had learned, or guessed, or thought elsewhere,
out of a simple act of lying together
meant for childbearing, not philosophy

nothing to do with human give and take,
things unconnected
with any of the modes of He and She,
pleasure, tenderness or company:
holes into Heisenberg, Blake or Eckhard's worlds
and these were seen, experienced, not thought –
later, too, not at the time, as if they were
conceived and grew: the last thing I'd expected
from that unacademic exercise.

Strange, how those Masters talking chastity
locked themselves in
and though industrious 'died in Cyprus
and so came never to Jerusalem'
or if they did, walked there in great lead boots
and made their dumb disciples do the same
wearing hair shirts and forced to travel on foot
lacking the Feminine Wings.

Those Elementary Inhabitants
all bachelors and virgins by profession
might have gone further if they took more risks
with reputation
or, having weakened for good human reasons,
in the act of penitence they'd have been amazed
at how much gain was there
and seen, great Solomon was nobody's fool

3

and women not the snares for Masterhood,
but more than human mothers, wives and friends –
openers of curtains upon Time
bringing us out of it, as well as in
having the gate between their thighs
themselves enlightened, knowing it or not,
since losing self is mixed into their pleasure
take us along with them

their bodies are the Masters' infant school.

Sir Thomas Allfraye, good courteous friend,
at eighteen years of age
married Elizabeth, Ambrose Comfort's child –
who lived with him until the end
in fifteen forty-nine, thirty-one years
(for wedlock was a serious business then,
not to be scratched out by a secular pen)
There were two children of the marriage.
Between his death and hers, she never smiled.
A hundred years after that came to pass
bigots removed his figure from the brass

leaving her there, the second time a widow,
while at her side his shadow
was worn away by godly feet.
And she, in hat and ruff, is praying still
neither content nor brokenhearted,
but that in God's good season
when such should be the heavenly will
tangibly and visibly arisen
good Christians, fearing no miscarriage,
remaining human, though sublime,

would as by assignation meet.
Though neither marrying nor given in marriage
they'd take the threads up where they parted
and have together the last laugh over Time.

Pope Innocent (may his undervalued yard
shrink to a pimple at the Resurrection)
first ruled the holy, celibate – and tarred
all subsequent Romans with that brush
shut up the spiritual window of the flesh
and all their contemplatives have been since one-eyed
wasting good time in getting mortified:
dan Moses saw and heard God in a bush,
thinking of his black Midianitish bride.

Luther took down the old weapon from the shelf,
accepted clerical marriage, frowned on lust.
It took us till now to brush off the dust.
Our generation's just declassified
the quickest way of seeing past the self
and rid it of the Puritan infection

but with so great a counselling chatter
Inferior Benevolence rules the matter
and flushes up another covey of fears.
Sexual seeing may room with human love
or it may not. The Indian seers
chose partners picking blouses from a pile

impersonal of deliberate intent
and separate from family ties –
not you and she, but He and She. Perhaps
in the pursuit of getting wise
we'll mould that use to our more tender style –
first you and I, then He and She,
then at will neither, though briefly
and opening other eyes
become more innocent than Innocent.

Old thinkers, bursting to explain
how what we see chimes with what's there,
lacking the necessary words, made this
model to tell what they saw, looking in:

'That God made one soul, which He split in two,
named them, and put them among the beasts and trees:
but they, having not much use for what was done
came naked together once more, skin to skin,
he in her, she around him –
and that whole world unmade itself again

'Then, that a snake broke in on their coition –
that she, picking the apple off the tree
(when they unwound, the tree was made again)
cut it in two, a red side and a green,
gave one to him and took the other.
The whole world splintered back to semblance then,
back into plants and tigers, years and days.
And still she cut it, again and yet again,
making a jealous God, the angel's sword,
birth, death and circumstances.' That's the story:

good, in default of algebra and field-theory
to plot what happened (Plato took it all
like a damned idiot, literally,
and saw the sexes orphaned halves
like guests who seek their partner at a party).
But there is this much solid in the tale

that each exconjugant held part of the other,
man in woman, woman in man.
The opus magnum is to put together
the couple, the whole apple
making diversity collapse again
setting the state of being as-you-were
for a while at least, to show a little
of the weave that makes the veil.

Soul to soul, mind to mind, both pleasant,
confuse the object of the exercise.
Body to body is the place to start.
And then with labour her dance can be unwound
the apple come together, and again
objects remelt and make a single ground
we see time's arrow endwise as a point –
things that those who have been there speak in figures
lacking the words to set them out in plain.

Ezekiel saw the bones arise –
four Living Things
whose life was linked to their eyed wheels –
Babylonian imaginings
informing ways of the mind.
The Jewish, literal, mould – I here, He there –
cracked open at some figure in a dream.
Perhaps the pylon-forms of kings
part-opened unaccustomed eyes

but through the intuition thrusts his head
the One God of externity
and roars out politics, and rites, and sin,
the kosher laws, the liturgy
invoking fire, in his God-awful voice
on various peccadilloes of the day:
and that din drove the eye-filled wheels away

It was too dangerous: Ezekiel threw
seeds of the Zohar back into the air
that they came from. Satan had put them there –
he clipped the visions to the shapes he knew,
set his prophetic mind to curse
unwanted insights of idolaters.

That Indian girl, standing under a tree,
has slipped out of her husband's house at night
holding her ornaments to keep them quiet.
Star-flowers, red and white,
fall from the branches in long constellations

singing, she was guided there by her own light –
listening – protests of the sleeping birds.
She's made a nuptial bed of leaves
in expectation of some lover.
Whom she expects there, Krishna or a man,

who she herself is – whether
gopi, adulteress or musical scale,
is not made plain: perhaps all three.
Lovers and visionaries and thieves
pursue with such great stealth their assignations:

John of Avila used the selfsame words
to figure God's encounter with his soul.

How can I not be bitter
   when I read the news
whom England gave the language
   that Ireland taught me use?

There is a madness drives us
   both back to that old cup
who thought at least our fathers
   had drunk the damned thing up

There's something in that liquor
   kills off sober thought,
six hundred years of folly
   drowned and going for naught

Our bigot mutual maxim
   that wrongs will bring out right
funds the old, profitless commerce –
   Long Kesh and dynamite

the same pigheaded policy
   trades fire with merciless pride –
Fusilier and Fianna
   still fall down side by side

and the ghost of shot MacDonough
   turns from the wall to front
the ghost of Earl Mountbatten
   standing on Rosses Point.

I've seen a friend, an Indian mathematician
bring home an egg-shaped stone he'd found
red-veined on a white milky ground,
dress it with flowers, pour butter on the thing
and use it as a mental stepping-stone
out of the middle-order frame of reference,
the cogito, time, and position:
because the white and red were He and She
in his traditional iconography
the stone could be a catalyst to the sense
that transformation of a field can bring
one out of many, objects out of One.
(Most of us present only saw a stone.)

Your new machine has cost ten millions from
the University: the music of the spheres
goes round and round in it and comes out where
lines and whorls on a dark plate
give you the wherewithal to meditate
on the same matter. It's a whacking sum

though other workers make good claims to have
got results sitting crosslegged outside a cave
by looking at the self which does the seeing –
such observation has to be confirmed.
Money's well spent that helps you comprehend

exactly what we mean by 'is' and 'being'.
You need to hit our culture on the head
with something very hard, to set it seeing
in any empathetic mode but one:
hard data would work better than a stone.

Tota Puri took a sharp spline of glass
and pushed it in between his pupil's eyes
to open them, let the homunculus out;
a relativistic world, from that onslaught,
came to be apprehended and not thought

The mat he sat on cost a couple of annas.
We have to look at such techniques as these -
we need all the assistance we can get
in monitoring the lenses we look through
or go on multiplying entities
until the particle-fanciers are weary.

Conjugating the irregular verb 'to know'
other researchers worked in other manners.
There are more ways to skin a cat than one,
and find the fine grain of that cogito –
chromodynamics and field theory
might come to profit before very long
from pouring butter on a piebald stone.

Forgive me, Graves, the Goddess is not white
her hair is long and black as jet
one can pass through her
as one passes through darkness

being more shadowy than light
when she stands in our way we may not see her
as dapple hides the leopard or the moth

nor does she frequent bright places –
when she addresses us it is from below,
from the base of the skull, from under ground
the wavelength of her brightness is outside
our eyes' compass. Therefore she is dark

Animists scared of ghosts see dark as evil
black is malign in iconography
it has become the livery of devils

not so: darkness is tender and belongs
to lovers, mothers, and the womb
it is the nursery-bed of dreams
the place where the roots grow:
the grave, of course, too, but she's Persephone
not Libitina, whom Eleusis honours,
the patroness of return. She's also Time:
muses and lemans are her deputies

one does not meet that goddess in sunlight.
Her darkness is not sentimental:
when she is terrifying, as she is,
dwelling, as she does, beside the funeral pyres,
she is saying 'Pass through my darkness, I am a gate:
if I drink blood, it is in play –
the sunshine world's a film which I have made –
you can leave the theatre: pass into my half-light
you will see better, you will forget time.'

Perhaps you saw her in her sunshine forms
the Young Maiden, or Stella Maris,
objects of transcendent knowledge both
but not the faces she turns to poetry

believe me, Graves, the Goddess is not white.

I think that once a hundred years
    the whole thing must be said again
in a form to fit the time
    although what's said remains the same

now things are thought that once were seen –
    the brain is made with left and right
and poets have the shortest cut
    between thinking and sight.

No help in looking back to those
    who jumped this course last time around:
things done once can't twice be done –
    we have to use what's now to hand.

We line up at the Masters' gate –
    Blake made the circuit perfectly:
and William Yeats had a firm seat
    but bogged down in theosophy.

Some others have a perfect round –
    gentle Julian of Norwich –
but all the long-faced saints who would
    have ridden better for a marriage

dressing up sight to fit their creeds
    knock down a pole, refuse a gate:
who gives a damn what they believed
    if they get the substance straight?

Swedenborg the engineer
    talked to spirits on the planets –
he and the monks saw some things clear,
    despite the buzzings in their bonnets

Blavatsky, Steiner, Gurdjieff
   and all the transcendental chatter –
who gives a monkey's for their thought?
   What they saw is all that matters.

Kant, with a very different seat,
   did his seeing through his thinking
and almost got Time by the throat –
   (his colleagues thought that he'd been drinking).

The Oriental masters, too
   who look so much more in command
sit on a different saddle – we
   must use the culture to our hand.

What all these saw is now being thought,
   and thought can be set out in plain –
after Mach and Heisenberg
   we need to write it all again.

Madame Moitessier
silk roses in her hair
a girl in a woman's dress

must have kept still for long
while Ingres did his work
catching the face, at least

and seeing herself remade
is serious, and inclined
to pout a little (I

would have liked to see her smile,
release that thick, black hair:
Ingres had other ideas

and all his women have
that engraved, French banknote face
even Angelica,

waiting to be redeemed
from the dragon in the story
gives way to his ideal)

a young wife dressed for the ball,
when we turn round to go
I think that she does too.

Leaving the dress and face
caught there, the girl herself
turning away, goes on

into the flow of time –
to Monsieur Moitessier
to children, change and dying.

She must have come back often
to look at that changeless thing,
a child in a woman's dress

one hand on locket and breast
the other holding a fan –
frozen while fashions changed

and she herself moved on.
Madame Moitessier
must have learned much about time.

Philosophers, psychoanalysts
sink separate wells or sit in barrels
their private waters over their feet
those single-system people

Nature and Mind, overdetermined both
assent to all that every school can pump
between their quarrels.
All private systems have some slice of truth

but their proprietors
over each hole erect a steeple
never both/and but either/or –
play-pools and internecine wars

the steamboat plies upon the river.

On the night-path to the cave portal
to the porous hill, hand in hand
he has the lantern, she the spool of thread
Knossos white as wax behind them
in front, the buried, pitiful bellowing
comes louder, then recedes

they pass shadowed entrances
she says 'Not those'. The path slopes down,
the arch is small, a darker cup of dark.
'This is the one,' she says.
'I have the lamp: you're not afraid, alone?'
'I have the Moon. Be quick.'

Between her fingers runs the thread. She feels
slow payings-out, tugs, hesitations,
heart in mouth when the line goes suddenly slack
then taut again, moving
the salmon's converse with the fisherman.

Does he know, I wonder (I did not tell him)
that every choice of ways gives one guess only,
closes when you have chosen – there is no
retracing? It is the thread alone defines the past.

Does he know, I wonder (I did not tell him)
it does not signify, which route one takes –
On the nonviable routes, we are not there:
there has to be a mind to hold the thread?

Does he know (I am sure he does not know)
that booming lamentation's just the air
which underground water carries into the hill?
Without a monster he would not go in.

And he had to go in – one has to be
born to become a hero. All we women
launch heroes from our wombs like paper boats
downstream. The thread records their choices

He holds one end. He thinks I hold the other.
We tie such threads to supple twigs and go,
So when he twitches it, it twitches back
reassurance. When he sees a lighter circle

and comes from shadow into brighter shadow
we're there to say 'What kept you then so long?'
and take him back into the womb.
Heroes are simple souls and content so

Provided only he does not sit down
at the point where the thread ends, and the porous
maze ahead is undetermined, at
the present (we call it 'present'), provided only

he does not stop, and stopping apprehend
suddenly how Daedalus designed
the thing – take the whole structure in
(there are some heroes of a different kind)

Then maze and thread and he and I will all
vanish along those other, forclosed, paths
already beyond reach. I do not think
this hero's of that stamp. I think he will

come out, shaking his sword, and boasting of
Pasiphae's terrible get he met and slew –
thought-forms, terrific thought-forms, bred in the dark
that kept his mind upon the straight and narrow

I hope he will do so – I want him back.

And even as she spoke, the thread went slack.

It was another copy that came out
shaking his sword and boasting it was done.
Thoughtful but unamazed she welcomed him
and when he spoke of Naxos, was content

even though she knew all, past and future,
even though she knew all, she said nothing.

A Palimpsest

Cleitophon and Leucippe, lovers in
an Alexandrian romance –
some tenth-century hand wrote out the story
to entertain its master and his girl:
with what success we have no evidence.

Parchment is costly, and that story not
given to edification. Brother Anselm
with pumice rubbed it out, as good as new,
and on the white page wrote the praises of
virginity. Time has a way with preaching –
in spite of Anselm, the old ink came through.

Not the whole text, but titillating fragments
between relentless lines of homily
(we have the story in another copy)
under the page, there is another page.

Fragments like these break in on us at times –
where was it? when? not in our life story,
but present, legible, in another hand:
incomplete deletion by some tide
takes out the footprints, but not all.

Arhats profess to read them – we cannot
unless black light brings the whole page to view –
but there are places, epicene fragments, names,
nothing as concrete as Euphorbus' shield
and under that page lies another page:
grassy thoughts, water, perhaps fear –
yes, the beast's voice from whom the parchment came

Past lives dug up by Californians
fail to convince – most of them make us royal.
These words between the lines are something else
born from the singular way we slice up Time.

'God sees Time,' Luther said, 'all of a heap' –
These are not things that happened once before
these things are happening, in other rooms

we multiply experience by i
a superposition, not a palimpsest.

The water's frozen, the birds are saying
nothing I want to hear
this is the time when one retrenches –
the butt-end of the year

each year, beginning England's winter
of barren heads and barren stalks
when summer looks a hopeless prospect
rockets salute Guy Fawkes

that paragon of demolition
token of getting one's own back
ratcatcher who set out to waste
the bastards at one crack

He failed of course: he may have been
framed, but he stands for the idea.
We lack the guts ourselves to try it
but each year, still, we cheer.

Most terrorists are stupid idiots
brainlessly blasting innocents,
doing their cause no good, devoid of
humour or commonsense

but one day soon, someone with brains
will send his wits to war –
not waste our nuclear clods, but show them
up for the pricks they are

There is not much to laugh about –
the state of England's not amusing
pig-people who root up our flowers
were our own choosing

I think the buggers underrate us:
a colony – it serves us right –
providing jobs as whores and waiters
(that is, if we are white)

Sickened with counterjumping grocers,
with daft old actors and their missiles
with big time villains lining pockets
it's time we blew some whistles

while vermin at the top dismantle
everything decent, popping corks,
still to the cause of getting even
we light our rockets for Guy Fawkes.

Each Spring, a spotted arum plant comes up
in the same place, under the apple, revenant,
identity in a new body present
a flame lit from a green flame

It makes a purple-cassocked preacher in
a jade pulpit shaped on the vesica piscis –
later, red berries to replenish birds:
then it is time to go, back into soil.

The plant is in the manifold we see
which made up Adam's garden and makes ours.
The link is in the underworld of roots
not in our frame, an Eleusinian mystery.

A minor model, this: the root is tangible,
can be dug up and taken in the hand,
and what springs up is fixed – repeatedly
itself, never a lichen or a rose

Good, though. We say 'Dust to dust, ashes to ashes' –
there are no arums stored somewhere in Heaven
but what comes on the stage must leave the stage,
what leaves the stage must enter in due time.

Unless it gains, meanwhile, Enlightenment,
next Spring it will be back.

Grandi believed that God
made all things that were made
out of a difference in phase
shifting the net of emptiness by one space –
so, out of nothing, something:
no substance, but a change of sign,

evidence of insubstantiality

John Wheeler says our thinking made the world –
stars, fossils, protons, dinosaurs, the lot:
the fox that comes and goes like a thin courtier,
grass, water, girls' breasts, and galaxies, old age

we make these things out of a pile of That –
they are our algorithms and not God's,
and making them we make their histories
even that fiery start of Space and Time

we were not there to see. We made these things,
footprints of children dancing on a shore

Some huge thing chimes with what John Wheeler says.

Large eyed and bald from chemotherapy
surrounded by enormous furry toys
he gets wheeled to the circus. Anything
to spin time out for him and stave off questions

but he's too wise to ask them. He can sense
how deeply death disturbs the adult world.
When they look red-eyed, he will try to help –
says he will go to sleep and wake with Jesus.

I would like to tell him (possibly he knows –
children have intuition beyond their years)
I would like to tell him he cannot fall off
the edge of a flat world, it is not like that:
explain, after each film the screen goes blank
briefly – say, with the Goddess, 'This game's over
Now we will play another'.

Curriculum Vitae

A fiend (they say) rode Mother while she slept
put into her his non-Euclidean
seed from outside our frame of reference.
Baptism bleached me, but not wholly:
some of the strange was kept.

First, I was born old and shall die a child.
You, clearly, see me living within the frame:
and yet, Sire, when your mind and my mind touch
there's something in me opposite in sign
walking against the stream of time

That whiff of alien seed did not insert
the complex conjugate, the mirror self,
which startles you with singularities –
it wrote no software which you have not got
it simply opens eyes.

Shamans are mirror-people. I am one.
Wizards are mirror-people in good standing,
counselling kings – not burned at stake or made
fodder for fieldwork, honoured not outcast
because their future is their past.

Vivien, with her bush, Nimue with her rock
thought they had fixed me. Coming back to peep
they said 'Merlin is sleeping'. But I was long gone.
From Then, those two moved forward, but I back
from this my powers come.

You say, my liege, there's now no social role
for mirror people. Those who see cube roots,
the musical, the double-jointed even,
have marketable skills, but we have none
the times being practical

I like to put my bunch of skills to work
helping my fellow men, correcting error.
Baptism put that in my head, I think.
You lack a counsellor. Beware, my liege,
Lest I hold up this mirror.

— O do not take my towel, Sir —
  let my garments be
I think a lady swimming
  deserves some privacy

— The water you're immersed in
  is privacy enough
I don't see ladies every day
  swimming in the buff

— You're certainly no gentleman
  to treat a woman so
You'd better turn your back at once
  I'll yell if you don't go

— The good God gave you, lady,
  a natural bathing suit —
come out and let me eyeball you
  from head to pretty foot

— I won't come out to you, Sir —
  you can come in to me
we can both be clothed in water
  with perfect modesty

— So why should we be modest
  to hide our honest skin?
You can stay where you are, my dear
  but I'm certainly coming in

— Strip off, strip off, the lady said,
  let me see if you're Alf or Ann
For every naked lady
  deserves a naked man

Three times he took her in the stream
    and three times on the land
and three times on the green, green grass
    till he could no longer stand

– Now cool it, cool it, lady fair:
    let the dog see the rabbit –
I need to take a breather now
    before you become a habit

– Then give me leave to get my wind
    and we will take our ease
and I will pick you apples two
    from these two apple trees

– You're something else, but there are things
    you never learned in college.
Yonder is the Tree of Life,
    and this the Tree of Knowledge

In water and upon the land
    we have wound back a clock.
– He said, I think I'd better go –
    I shall be late for work.

– O Sir, the trains that brought you here
    have run beyond your reach.
He tumbles from the frame of time
    who nine times lays a witch.

And you can run as best you may
    until you break your heart
like an ant in a Klein bottle
    you'll finish where you start

for here your East is joined to West,
    your North is joined to South
inside a singularity
    not even light gets out.

Then he became a running fox
    and she became a hound
and far and wide in the greenwood
    she followed him to ground.

She's rowed him in her cloth of gold
    and set him down to sleep
and she has turned his pager off
    for fear that it should beep.

So he became a sleeping man
    and she became a dream
He woke to see a naked girl
    a-swimming in the stream.

Fish have the look of people. Eyes and mouth
are roughly where our own are: fish have masks,
seem to be persons. They have not much mind,
their heads, cut off, continue swallowing.
Alive and on the move, one sees in them
aunts, uncles, neighbours, characters from life
the fat old chap, the predator, the belle.
Catching them, too, one feels that one has caught
desperate people who can make no sound
are pitifully voiceless, even dying.

I get no pleasure out of catching fish.

Not sentiment, this, but empathy
a twitch on some thread in the Elsewhere which
joins my mind to a colder mind. Somewhere

the speechless rightness of possessing scales,
a wrinkling sky of water: very terrible
and strange suddenly to drown in air.
One cannot say much more about such things –
I get no pleasure out of catching fish.

With us, the skeleton has few friends
only the priest and the anatomist. One
produces it at our feasts, an awful warning
unless of course we at once return to God:
the other appreciates its striking beauty.

In the Middle Ages, flesh was more transparent
skeletons danced at weddings, reaped, occupied thrones
tokens of the equality of flesh which is grass.
Now they are more like concrete ghosts – appearing
they indicate tomb-robbers, or wilful murder.

It is indecent to refer to them –
after all, we understand the real world,
the cogitating mind has proved to us
skeletons survive but it does not.
Memento mori only rubs it in

Except in Mexico: skeletons there
are seen and domestic – children play with them
sugar skulls, little coffins
each with its occupant. In prints,
skeleton mariachis play.

In part, no doubt, this is the Catholic church
part is much older, the defeated gods
counterattacking. Part
is another view of the real world
derived from cactus-juice, not physics

in which the 'I' is neither ghostly nor spiritual
in which the mind outranks the tangible order
in which the mind outlasts the skeleton
because it makes the tangible unreal world.

Some recent work suggests they may be right.
Skulls have an awkward way of asking questions
and this is one we have not sorted out.

I cannot say that I set out –
once on the road there is no stopping:
somehow, about the age of two,
I found myself alive and walking

between my parents, on a road,
aware of other travelling figures
some were relations, others not
my parents rarely talked to strangers

the road was wet and uniform
I did not ask where we were going
one concentrates on keeping warm
there did not seem much point in knowing

At seven I took a bypath through
a couple of disastrous schools –
when that was over, Mother taught
me as we trudged. I learned the rules –

press on regardless, damn the shells,
(it took a while for that to show)
my mother introduced me to
a gentleman called Cyrano

who made a very great impression
(one looks for role models at seven)
There was one thing I learned –
that knowing things can get you even.

At twelve, I plodded off alone
got separated from the party
worked hard at lessons, and acquired
a mortal dread of Nobodaddy

from some tendentious Bible class
my parents watched in consternation
God-merchants always take their chance
when one discovers masturbation.

When the rain stopped, I knew the next
town on the route prescribed was Learning
a Cyrano requires a blade –
I picked that one, and took the turning

the road was arduous but pleasant
the scenery extremely fine
they give you points over this section
and at the checkpoint I got mine

Luckier than other travellers, who
fell over cliffs or into marshes –
a staff and snake, a bag of skills,
and now the march was its own purpose

I missed a lot – I did not have
to be so bloody singleminded
girls, for example: they were like
expensive fruit, and best avoided

though marvellous as a table centre
and salivatingly displayed
one stiffened, but could not believe
that they could actually be laid

Back on the main road, then, with pleasure
tending the fallen as I tramped
(a wife and child now walked alongside –
I'd bingoed at the first attempt)

We camped in various locations
with travellers we'd got to know
medicine made me ask the question
'Where does this bloody journey go?'

I fixed the breakdowns, oiled the joints
I buried those who didn't make it
One can't help starting to explore
the meaning of the one way ticket

a road consists of destinations
when you fall out, it means you're there
all pilgrims set out with a target
but tourists end up anywhere

It was a nice but shapeless walk
if pilgrimage was in abeyance
I felt a map would help: I took
the track which led to Natural Science

pushing a quite substantial cart
loaded with various sorts of booty.
Counting the miles we'd done one night
I suddenly found that I was forty

Intent upon the pilgrim thing
I'd bypassed all the main attractions
and taken pride in making up
time over the most difficult sections.

At fifty years, I trudged between
two women, in atrocious weather
shared my oilskins with one, and found
when the sky cleared, we were together

I did towns now which, when a prig,
I never would have dared to visit
they needed seeing – but I got
a wholly unexpected profit

among the gimcracks in the cart
the intellectual and the horny
somewhere, I found, I had picked up
a guidebook to this whole weird journey

perhaps I bought the thing, or pinched it
in a hotel from off a shelf
could be, an offbeat Gideon Bible –
perhaps I wrote the thing myself.

Science is much like Nobodaddy
step out of line, and you're a Charlie:
I kept the guidebook in brown paper
and talked about it rather rarely –

started to walk with physicists
(they are all Charlies by profession)
and found they'd read the thing already:
they'd got it from mathematicians

We soon became a marching column
all sorts of curious types latched on
my colleagues called us Falstaff's Army
and left us studiously alone

a mystic and a Trappist monk
two yogis and a statistician
(I'd like some more biologists)
the walk's become an expedition

the physicists have gone ahead
to hire some transport for their gear
the track ahead runs steeply up
we shall camp late since the night's clear

what do we think? The road's a circle,
a trot around a closed dimension
and wholly virtual anyway
a mathematical convention

dissolved by spinors and low cunning
or meditating on a mat
or, if you'd rather, apparatus
designed for laying hold on That

hardly a pilgrimage, you'd say
the signpost to this track said 'Science:
impracticable for vehicles'
you need to work, not hold a seance

Here come the physicists at last
two yaks, three pony-loads of gear.
The walk has been well worth the blisters –
I'm interested how I came here.

We say, there is an end to everything –
there'll be a last time that the moon will rise
even a last time that we lie together

(first one and then the other, Fitzgerald said)

Final occasions happen unannounced
they do not put up signs
for gradual or for sudden lastnesses

but then these things are unreal anyway
they simply are. We make things 'first' or 'last':
Time's how our heads work – so is Sequence:
First Luther, then De Broglie, made the point –
God sees such firsts and lasts all of a heap.
What's real is the coherent superposition.

The Englishman's Dartry Walk

A dead whale's bones that whistled
on the strand at Lissadell
made the first harp, they say.
It is a powerful spot –
one can't discount the tale –
a place that takes to school
whether we like or not.
I first came to Ireland
when I was young, to learn
obstetrics and not verse.
No kind of Celt myself
(old Comforts came from Kent
where the Normans set their boot)
and I was altered much
walking along the stones
where whalebone turns to song
and learning from that ground
what Yeats was talking about
and all his ancestry.

You'd say, 'he's a soft touch.
Platoons of Englishmen
were enthused over pishogues
while they beat Ireland down.'

True, that – but there's more:
no sentiment, believe me,
no mists and mysteries.
Instruction that I got
came thought the soles of my feet –
those sensible pedal-notes
in hillsides, just below
the pitch of audible sound
that run below the ground
could well make beached bones sing.
No doubt the inhabitants

get used to them. I could hear.
There's information focused
in those hills' singular forms
that schools if one is apt
even an alien
who had no notion walking
that he had come to school
and learn to thrust his thumb
through the Middle Order veil.
Perhaps that place is strong
because the veil is thin
and there's a white hole here,
a singularity
that drives that pedal-note,
a different algebra
which alters how we write:
history comes later,
knowledge last of all.

I

'Irish poets, learn your trade . . .'
God's feet, am I disqualified
from taking that man's wise advice
being born and bred on the other side,
and with no decent standing-place
except this language that we share?
Poetry's neither here nor there –

Ireland and India both have laid
a hand upon me, and it shows.
I myself, being so taught,
read Ireland's hills with India's thought
and cannot put the touch away.
Both have their catalogues of woes
marked 'made in England' – shameful stuff
but not to be hung around my neck.
It's not our poets who should pay
for the stinkers of their kind.
England has had woes enough
laid on us by the selfsame scum,
the common curses of mankind:
now foreign wars being out of stock
they fix attention nearer home
and turn their venom on their own
the Colonel's lady and the Squire –
that grocer cailleach on her seat
dreams of the Tans and General Dyer
teaching the Working Class a lesson –
suckling a toad at each dry teat.
We have no call to make confession:

Poets, I think, are on one side
and haters of the things you hate –
nooky with Reagan, tea with Botha,
lies and colonial police.
That anger is a source of pride
the best credential of a brother:
we do not need to make our peace.

And poetry does not stop there.
I think of Rowan Hamilton
scratching the thing that he had seen
on the stone coping of a bridge.
The thing that he had written down
bears on the nature of What Is —
hypercomplex not tuneful numbers
but cousin still to poetry.
Yeats' dancer by the edge
of a waveless sea is myth, not math;
the mystic, coming back, remembers
and both address the same strange thing
belong in one anthology
having walked a common path.

These judge from verses we have made
how soundly we have learned our trade.

II

Coming down Glencar by the lesser road
between the hurrying lake and the wet fern
you see the lion couched there in the hill
perfect of eye and ear and mane
and grey as if he carried dust.
No use to mount on the grey paw
and question him. Coming abreast he's gone
changed from a beast to that enormous plow
pointing its furrow at Grange. All round
other grey numinous beings less defined
at every corner of the hill a beast
not fully realized as the lion is
but buried, hinted at, and living.
From the four corners of the hill
great beasts of the Apocalypse
look out, withdrawing as you pass.
Seers are mastered by the landscape here —
why should a rocky shape forshadow That
like formulae or iconography

or a woman's tossing body? They set forth
perfectly Substance and Becoming –
chopped out of stone by moving ice
and a parabola of screes
haecceitas of the stone, and hence in part
a large substance, not expressible,
of whose thisness this is.
The old monks on Inishmurray droning prayer
looked up and saw, slate-carved below fat clouds
the unmoving pagan beasts still in their places.
Their times were violent, like ours –
something (they crossed themselves) was passing over
threatening an apocalypse not God's
and letting loose the beasts within the hill
those august beasts, incensed against mankind
shaken out of sleeping by a race without
chastity, honour or regard for times
which God forbid. They crossed themselves again –
their task was to keep such things bottled up.

Well, Lion, there's no war here any more:
Ulster is boiling to the North –
Mountbatten died here: that was yesterday –
others have died: that too was yesterday.
Old Celtic heroes played the honest ruffian
but that was yesterday in spades.
We make those beasts into apocalypse
out of our fears. That's not what they are saying.
The threatening footsteps are humanity's.
They meditate, those stone philosophers,
upon the human choice of universes
which are not the universes that they see –
on the world-line where they are living beasts
and on the virtualness of flowing time.
Questioned, in voices like an organpipe
they say 'If you look, you will see it too'.

48

III

They say that Rowan Hamilton
  with his wife was walking
by the canal, as such men do
  thinking as well as talking

one half his skull being taken up
  with harmless conversation
one half was grinding models of
  vectors in rotation.

There was a reed stood by itself
  a frog's jump from the meadow:
on the brown canal it cast
  reflection and a shadow

and that reed whistled in his ear
  'there is a thing to try –
Do i then j is not the same
  as doing j, then i'.

Mrs Hamilton, good soul,
  knew well the signs no doubt
and held her peace upon his arm
  waiting what might come out

and coming just then to the bridge
  she saw himself sit down
and scratch the rules for i, j, k
  upon the coping-stone.

There is an elegant tablet now
  where that idea took root
how vectors are not soldiers' feet:
  their drill does not commute.

It was a handy calculus
   which was written there.
Meantime, in the painted world
   appeared a minute tear.

The tear was small, the paint like life,
   and the backcloth sound.
Nobody put his eye to it
   to see what lay beyond.

The world was real in '43
   when men knew white from black –
That little tear had not let in
   Neils Bohr and Dirac

physicists were solid men,
   not wild as drunken sailors.
But the tune the reed had whistled was
   The Devil Among the Tailors.

A toast to Rowan Hamilton
   who set the rot afoot
a toast as well to i, j, k
   that they do not commute:

to grasp the mirrorness of things
   we like a calculus.
Being a poet, I myself
   see it as Merlin's glass

or that which the Goddess holds up
   for her square Spouse to see
where One turns Many, and the shards
   make our reality.

IV

Try talking physics to a solid man:
this old one's spent his life in raising calves
and listening to the priest, with reservations.
'Tell me,' says he, 'how you men see the world'
and stares me out to match my stick with his.
I say, it seems the real's a video game
played on a screen, and the real stuff's elsewhere.
'Ah yes,' says he, 'Hannon's have got one in –
there's a small world in that, with its own rules.
I waste no money on it, but I watch:
you see the boyos shooting rockets down.
If my being here's a game, we are inside it:
I once remarked as much to Father Carr –
Father, you think God thinks the way you think,
I said. He thinks I'm an old codger, so.'
John Jameson and porter, sip on sip . . .

So I go on and talk about world lines –
that everything occurs which can, but we
wear blinkers that shut out to left and right.
'It's mad enough,' says he, 'to be the truth.
If Time's codology, are we born and buried?
We think we are, and this is market day –
seen from the side, all that lies in a heap.'

We take a quick run round the place of Mind,
The old one says 'This I have always thought –
the mind that was Cuchulainn walks somewhere,
possibly in the likeness of a girl:
if it were you or me, we'd never know.
All gets made new. The weapons are hung up,
the bones disposed in one of many mounds,
there's nothing strange in it. There's only Now;
and Then and After are just names we fix
just as a matter of convenience
on slices cut by our peculiar heads
on what's a solid, undivided stuff.

51

That's what your friends are saying? It's the truth
and makes elegant good sense to me,' the old man says.
He fumbles in his jacket and brings out
a wad of money that's seen many days.
'In spite of which,' says he, 'it's time to march –
game or no game, we have to play it, so.
It's calves I came about, and that's the game.
Wisdom won't pay the mortgage. I'll drink up.
Philosophy's a fine and powerful thing,
too much of which could have a man destroyed;
Like whiskey, is it?' Rising from his chair
he claps his hat down on the Implicate.

V

It was forty years ago
I came over this hill
walking to Cliffoney.
Looking down from stones
and the black turf I saw
the hollow corrie of crags
and the road of the Horseshoe was
a winding thread that passed
a grey and broken house
blind windows on two floors
matchbox sized below me –
a long way off, the sea.
Troublesome, the path down.

It is still so, still silent
the black arena of crags
at whose crest spring up
the rushing skeins of mist.
A ragged arch looks down –
'Dermot and Grania's bed'
an arduous bed to reach
save for the dots of sheep
on screes too steep for standing.

In the rushing mist of a chimney
the merry ravens dance.

The bones they have picked clean
by Palmerston's ferny walls
have yielded ghosts to the wind –
ghosts of sheep, these.
Are they alone, the sheep,
a many-throated bleating
changed to the hissing of streams?
There may be others present
whom the dancing birds remember
or are made birds themselves

McNeill's and Devin's ghosts
who left the armoured car
down there, by the sheep's ruin
an ambush had unroofed
when, seeing a blind end,
they climbed the boggy path
by Palmerston's old walls.
Rifles were waiting there –
how at each round in that soundingboard
the cliffs bellowed, ravens rose!

Not only those, perhaps.
I think I would look here
for those two unforgiven
ghosts who set all afoot,
on whom ghosts turn their backs:
he silent, she professing
in the hiss of the streams
'It was so small a thing –
and we had love taken,
that takes away the brain.
How could we know the harm?'

Whisht, whisht, Devorgilla –
I hear another voice,

the Lion in the hill,
'If you are looking for ghosts
they are of deeds, not men,
of dying, not of the dead –
sniper's and target's thoughts:
what thought them is elsewhere
dressed now in other clothes.
The old array hangs here –
and well they are rid of it.
Even your unforgiven
being in new clothes, forget
what there was to forgive.

'They go to poets' heads,
those rags that hang on the bush.
There's nothing ghostly here
but Adam's trick with time
in making Here and Now,
those weird coordinates
which hacked me from a hill.
Did he scratch all that on a bridge
in Eden, while his wife
stood by, one hand behind her,
holding the stolen fruit?
Well, you should know, not I –
it was he who set the rules.'

He should know too, that beast
who once was a sea-bed
and will be so once more
The rags of deeds that hang
on the cliff, would I know them again
if I had worn them once?

Woman of the Red-headed Man

It was a morning we were early stirring
when without asking our two paths joined
neither intending to make a meeting
but each one reading the other's mind

It was soft day, a Sunday evening
the sun was set and the hedges blind
no vows were taken, no word was spoken
but each knew surely the other's mind

Foot of the sallow, the noisy curlew —
we had no need then of roof or bed.
These have not altered but all is altered
I was not banned then, you still unwed

When I lie waking you're likely sleeping
with holy sanction you've been laid to rest
that bright hair wedded, both dead and buried
with a stranger's fingers about each breast.

I dreamed about a house and lands
that were not mine. Those folk were gone –
some of them clearly buried there

since under old and peaceful trees
were marble crosses in a row:
no surnames anywhere on the stone

they by their presence seemed to be
passing responsibility.

I did not go inside the house.
It's an odd patrimony, and not mine –
Later, perhaps. Or in another time.

Once it was dancing – I remember that:
books, records, practice in a village hall,
pink gauze, two middle-aged professionals:
that passed, in time. I can still dance.

Again, roses; another time it was roses –
those new and old names in the catalogues
the genealogies of all the names
species, rosa mundi.
That was in the past. The books are on the shelf.

Languages, too – Russian, Sanskrit, Morse,
these things one dehydrates, puts in store.
They can be broken out when needed
after some dusting and revision.
The name of it is learning and part-forgetting

they go to store: what stays is metaknowledge
all those doors stay unlocked: one should ignore
the voice which says 'you will be tested on this'.
Be quiet boy. I am seventy years of age.

He is the senior beast, the eldest.
Sailing by Catalina, his white breath
sits on the flanks of a long swell.
He has seen everything: older and younger brothers,
the right, the sperm, the sei and the great blue
for centuries the traffic of the sea
those mighty, gentle skulls –
when they died, he swam deeper
avoiding shipping lanes; his sonar tasted
the unfamiliar babel in the sea.

What notions are there now in that broad head?
Obeying his sealed orders, never late
in the sea of Cortez, in the green Arctic –
they will swim northward, all his docile children,
and some of them will get through. He has no feuds,
not with the iron, not with us;
he has done what he must. There will still be
jawbones to make the arch at the ranch gate.
He does not know yet he has made us friends.

We want no dead weights on this expedition,
no credulous Charlies and no nervous Nellies.
Though not as hazardous as in the past
the intellectual skulls you see down there
all fell from this arête. So use some care –
look out and in, don't try to go too fast,
but climb, Goddamit, don't crawl on your bellies.

The particle physicist and the mathematician
I'll take. They're crazy, but they watch their feet.
I'll take one mystic – no, not you, Ouspensky,
nor you, Teilhard. You've got no head for heights.
What do you say, Sherpa? Very well, we'll take
two at the most – Eckhard and William Blake,
and watch it, you two – no religious fights.
I need a brain man, too (he's got the map
and the theodolite). You others, don't
for Christ's sake hold us up with poking for
the Absolute and Transcendent (you'll see plenty
of that keeping the rope taut, eyes front)
or any other Rosicrucian crap.
People who play games on this pass
end on a slab with parsley up their ass:
that was what put paid to those skulls down there.

Remember you've two feet, one left one right.
Now, if you're ready, we'll leave at zero twenty
that is, unless there are more fool suggestions.
The sherpa's name is Mi Pham. He's our guide.
Now, get those bloody packs on. Any questions?

When Philip Gosse set out to square
The Bible with geology
He reasoned, Adam had a navel
So even God's not able
To make a piece without a history

And he could salvage the inerrant Word –
Each creature had an umbilical cord
Of fossils, ancestors and evolution
Supplied as extras. That's why things were there.
It seemed to him an elegant solution –
Charles Kingsley found the whole idea absurd.

It never struck them God might not see time
Quite the way we do, from Kant's a prioris,
Or even be a believer in First Causes:
You simply for 'casuality' write 'being' –
The myth of sequence is in our display.
Gosse's contortions struck his age as lame,
A blend of pat duplicity and unction:
They look much less so in a quantum frame.
Our heads rotate time to a real dimension
Making This follow That, a neat convention
If you can't process uncollapsed state-functions –
A transcomputable world must still be lived in.
We leave 'what is' to particle-collectors
With twistors, matrix algebra and bi-vectors
And then find out, some tiresome eremite
By gazing at his navel got it right.

That was the year that Newton left Great Court
and our twice-striking clock to rescue Sterling –
a practical concern, like bodies falling,
or reckoning Time at sea:
but he came back, when currency allowed,
and worked behind the leaded, bowed
Trinity windows up one flight
in eye-destroying candle light
on problems of another sort –
how Number makes things hold together.
Could counting Hebrew letters be a key?

He was too early for space-time, too late
for the Kabbalah, Dee, and Michael Maier,
and settled for Reduction, of the sort
that set our style of knowing until today.
Roubilliac's statue catches him, on the point
of seeing how things come together –
grasping for some plain words to integrate
what we see with what is there
and pull coherence from it all,
but still the apple will not fall.

Some of it was Pythagoras, who came
closer than most, and some
the alchemical mishmash which combined
Hermes, freemasons, Jung and Revelations
into a soufflé which turns off the mind:
where to begin on that? Not with equations.
Yet every soufflé has an egg in it:
it took two hundred years to get
the yolk of that egg back into its shell.

The apple story's myth. Nevertheless
Newton some time and somewhere must have seen
if not an apple fall, then something else
to form the image of the World Machine.
Genius moves by seeing, not by thought.
Some time, somewhere, maybe in Trinity

with the twice-striking clock, or another place
where there's a double-take of Time
like Leibnitz, or Descartes who dipped

his Catholic toe in meditation,
and from then on was troubled by the 'I',
Pythagoras seeing the ripples in a pail –
Newton had got the message – could not get
words to set it out in print:
somewhere between the planets and the Mint
he'd tripped over a corner of the Veil.

Marconi's sputtering spark transmitter
which charged wire fences and gave cows a jolt
in nineteen-one sent out a string of S's –
they copied him in Saint John's, Newfoundland.

Eighty-four light years out, they journey on
like the Three Kings, those dots, between the stars.
To them it seems they took no time at all
seeing that photons lack a sense of time –
instantly there. To us it looks like years.

There is no past – or rather, there's no present:
'Present' is something of a human joke,
the moving dot where the con-trail begins.
A being of imaginary mass
could overtake Marconi's plodding dots
and his con-trail would stream forward, not back.

You have long known I have to come
knocking at your most recent door:
I am unwelcome but not strange
We have so often met before

I am that officer by night
who tells you to evacuate
take nothing with you, good or bad –
no, you alone. I will not wait.

Such knocking never welcome is
They show no gratitude to me.
It is most needful that I press
the key erasing memory –

wasteful, perhaps, to spill so much,
but there are matters to forget.
Think: it could be at Paschendaele
or Buchenwald that we last met

and all those earlier strands of time
would be too much, retaining all:
each passage has its share of wounds –
against those I erect a wall

mask and garments will be new
(what you abandon is well worn)
and with no memory of me
or what transpired, or being born

waking into some other part
you'll not recall the closing door,
expect my knocking, and deny
that you and I have met before.

Also available from Sinclair-Stevenson

MARTYN CRUCEFIX

On Whistler Mountain

With the publication of his first collection, *Beneath Tremendous Rain*, Martyn Crucefix was acclaimed as an 'incisive new voice' (*The Times*) and 'an outstanding talent from whom great things can be expected' (Herbert Lomas/*Ambit*). His poetry was praised as 'distinctive' and 'richly enjoyable' (*TLS*), capable of 'fusing lush sensuality with a bred-in-the-bone seriousness' (*City Limits*).

Crucefix's new collection, *On Whistler Mountain*, builds on this success. Here, the dead re-visit the living; a lover flies on real dove's wings; an old soldier dreams he is one of the Magi; a computer programmer suffers a terrifying haunting. Wide-ranging, vivid and powerful, these poems leap sometimes shockingly, sometimes delightfully, into secular vision and, in doing so, extend the imaginative remit of contemporary poetry.

MARTYN CRUCEFIX won a major Eric Gregory award in 1984, a Hawthornden Fellowship in 1991, and has had poems published widely and broadcast on BBC Radio 3. His first collection, *Beneath Tremendous Rain* (1990), was published by Enitharmon Press.

ANTHONY THWAITE

The Dust of the World

The poems in Anthony Thwaite's new book range from Japan, a country he has known well since 1955, to the United States, where he spent part of a wartime childhood and to which he has returned several times. In between come poems drawing on Yugoslavia, Iraq, India, elegies for poet friends (George MacBeth, Philip Larkin, George Barker, Howard Nemerov) and some indefinable poems of search, loss, regret, and wonder.

By turns witty, desolate, acute and accurate, these are the poems of someone who is always probing for the nerve of his memories and his experiences. This is Thwaite's eleventh book of poems; it follows his *Poems 1953–1988*, published in 1989.

ANTHONY THWAITE was born in 1930. He has been a university teacher in Japan and Libya, literary editor of *The Listener* and *New Statesman*, and co-editor of *Encounter* 1973–1985. He has been the recipient of the Richard Hillary Memorial Prize, a Cholmondeley Award, and the O.B.E.

JAMES MICHIE

Collected Poems

This collection includes some entirely new poems, as well as selections from past books and magazine publications. Some of Michie's translations also feature, particularly of Théophile Gautier's work.

'Extraordinarily good, a harvest of some of the most inventive and memorable light verse of our time.' Peter Porter, reviewing *New and Selected Poems*.

JAMES MICHIE's poetry was first published in *Penguin New Writing* in 1950. Since then his work has appeared regularly in magazines on both sides of the Atlantic and in anthologies, notably W H Auden's *A Certain World* and Philip Larkin's *The Oxford Book of Twentieth-Century English Verse*. He is also well known for his verse translations of classical poetry.

ALAN BROWNJOHN

In the Cruel Arcade

In the Cruel Arcade, Alan Brownjohn's ninth volume of verse, is one of the most substantial and varied of all his collections, impressively wide-ranging in its themes and displaying an assured command of both regular and free verse forms. The title derives from a haunting poem about a childhood nightmare of birth and death, recalled in later life. It occurs in the first of the book's three sections where, by direct or indirect allusion, the poems trace in sequence a process of illness and recovery. The mood can be chilling; but it is leavened with this poet's characteristic wit and irony. The second section contains some moving poems of nostalgia and loss, and others sharply registering social and political change. The third develops the themes of the first two sections and adds a dimension of disarming fantasy and satire. *In the Cruel Arcade* has all the humour, formal elegance and surprise which admirers of Alan Brownjohn's writing have come to expect.

ALAN BROWNJOHN's most recent book of poems was *The Observation Car* (1990). His novel, *The Way You Tell Them*, won the Author's Club prize for the best first novel of 1990.

RUTH FAINLIGHT

This Time of Year

In a study of Ruth Fainlight's work, Barbara Hardy has written: 'She moves through the world of daily surfaces, objects and encounters, contemplating the ordinary, trying to be alert and not waste or be vague about experience . . . making dailiness strange, exotic and demanding . . .'

There is a note of irony and humour in Ruth Fainlight's new collection which has not been heard before. While the subjects of these poems range from political terrorism to the giant Pacific octopus to the Sibyls of the classical world, the book's title-poem, 'This Time of Year', confirms the deepening emotional resonance of her more personal poems, and a further development of technical and linguistic skills.

RUTH FAINLIGHT has published eight collections of poems – most recently *The Knot* – and a 'Selected', as well as pamphlets and folios from private presses.

JON SILKIN

Selected Poems

Jon Silkin's *Selected Poems* draws on his nine collections of verse, beginning with *The Peaceable Kingdom* (1954), but does not include anything from his most recent collection, *The Lens-Breakers* (1992).

Of his *Selected Poems*, first published in 1980, and now enlarged, the *TLS* wrote: 'Silkin has gone on developing: from being a poet who had done some fine things he has became a fine poet'. Here is a rich collection of poetry which deals with important human themes, including compassion, love and the face of evil.

JON SILKIN's most recent collection of verse is *The Lens-Breakers* (Sinclair-Stevenson, 1992). His collection of verse, *Nature With Man*, was awarded the Geoffrey Faber Memorial Prize in 1966. He and his wife co-edit *Stand*, a literary quarterly. He is a fellow of the Royal Society of Literature.